Contemplations
to be or not to be

Musings

Reflections

&

Surmisings

william s. peters, sr.

Inner Child Press International
'building bridges of cultural understanding'

Credits

Author

William S. Peters, Sr.

Editor

hülya n. yılmaz, Ph.D.

Cover Design

William S. Peters, Sr.
Inner Child Press International`

General Information

Contemplations
William S. Peters, Sr.

1st Edition: 2024

This publishing is protected under Copyright Law as a "Collection". All rights for all submissions are retained by the individual author and/or artist. No part of this publishing may be reproduced, transferred in any manner without the prior WRITTEN CONSENT of the "Material Owner" or its representative, Inner Child Press. Any such violation infringes upon the creative and intellectual property of the owner pursuant to international and federal copyright law. Any queries pertaining to this "Collection" should be addressed to the publisher of record.

Publisher Information:

Inner Child Press
intouch@innerchildpress.com
www.innerchildpress.com

This Collection is protected under U.S. and International Copyright Laws.

Copyright © 2024: William S. Peters, Sr.

ISBN-13: 978-1-961498-28-0 (inner child press, ltd.)

$ 21.95

Poets, Writers . . . know that we are the enchanting magicians that nourishes the seeds of dreams and thoughts . . . it is our words that entice the hearts and minds of others to believe there is something grand about the possibilities that life has to offer and our words tease it forth into action . . . for you are the Poet, the Writer to whom the Gift of Words has been entrusted . . .

~ wsp

for those who choose

to think,

to consider,

to dream,

and to rebel.

Table of Contents

Preface   *xiii*

The Poetry and the Prose

A Plea for Our Humanity	3
A Poem in the Making	5
For the People	8
You Can't Drink the Ocean	11
Meandering	12
A Letter from Joy	14
Going to the Light	15
A House on Fire	17
Self	19
Crossing Au Naturel	20
I Am a Book	22
A World of Seekers	24
I Believe	26
A Poem I Wrote Today	28
My Heart Throbs	30

Table of Contents . . . *continued*

All Because of Freshly Cut Grass	32
The Quietude	35
Small Things	36
Gratefulness	37
And I Breathe	38
Loved	41
An Interview with Death	42
Pondering	46
I Just Smile	47
As a Writer	49
Waiting	50
A Rose Is Still a Rose	52
I Am but a Seed	54
Good Morning!	56
Quick Enough	57
Slaves	59
A Sunday Morning Reflection	60
The Fruits of Trust	63

Table of Contents... *continued*

If I Could . . .	65
Me and Thee	67
Just an Ordinary Reflection	70
As the Brilliance Fades	73
The Journey	76
I Dance	77
The Magic	79
Perspectives	80
A Conundrum	81
Who Knows?	83
The Making of Jesus	85
Could Be . . .	90
Sprung	92
It's All Good	94
Acceptable	96
Those Days	97
Being Reflective	99
To Be or Not to Be	100

Table of Contents ... *continued*

Samsara	103
Minor Distractions	105
The Cauldron	107
Unfortunately	109
You	111
See You in Sinop	114
We Do What We Can	116
The Phoenix	119
Whether ...	120
Alone	121
Embracing the Wind	123
To What End?	125
Being Human	127
Just Another Day	129
Notes	130
A Reality Check	131
Gardeners	132
There Will Be Days ...	134

Table of Contents ... *continued*

You Get What You Give	135
Simple Gestures	138
I Dream a Little	139
When We Sang Along	141
On Me	143
Love Warriors	145

Epilogue

About William S. Peters, Sr.	149
A Selection of Other Works by the Author	155
Web Links of the Author	175

Preface

I am a believer!

Everything has a purpose. Sometimes this thing we term "purpose" is clear, but I believe, most times it is ambiguous. When I consider my own personal purpose, I conclude that expressing those things that trigger my consciousness, my soul, my spirit to be the catalyst of my purpose. Was I born to write? Who knows? Is there an end game to the direction I chose to go? Again, who knows? All I do know is that it is quite meaningful and fulfilling for me to express the things that stir me, inspire me, compel me to share my thoughts and feelings which manifest through me via what I like to note as my Muses.

In this hodge-podge of expression, you will find many things spoken in word that emanate from a myriad of direction. As I said in my 'dedication', this book is for those who choose to think, to consider, to dream, and to rebel. I think you will discover in your reading that this premise holds true ... either that, or I am deluded and 'full of my self'! At any rate, I hope that you, the reader, do glean something of significance from my offering.

Bless Up

Bill

The Poetry

&

The Prose

william s. peters, sr.

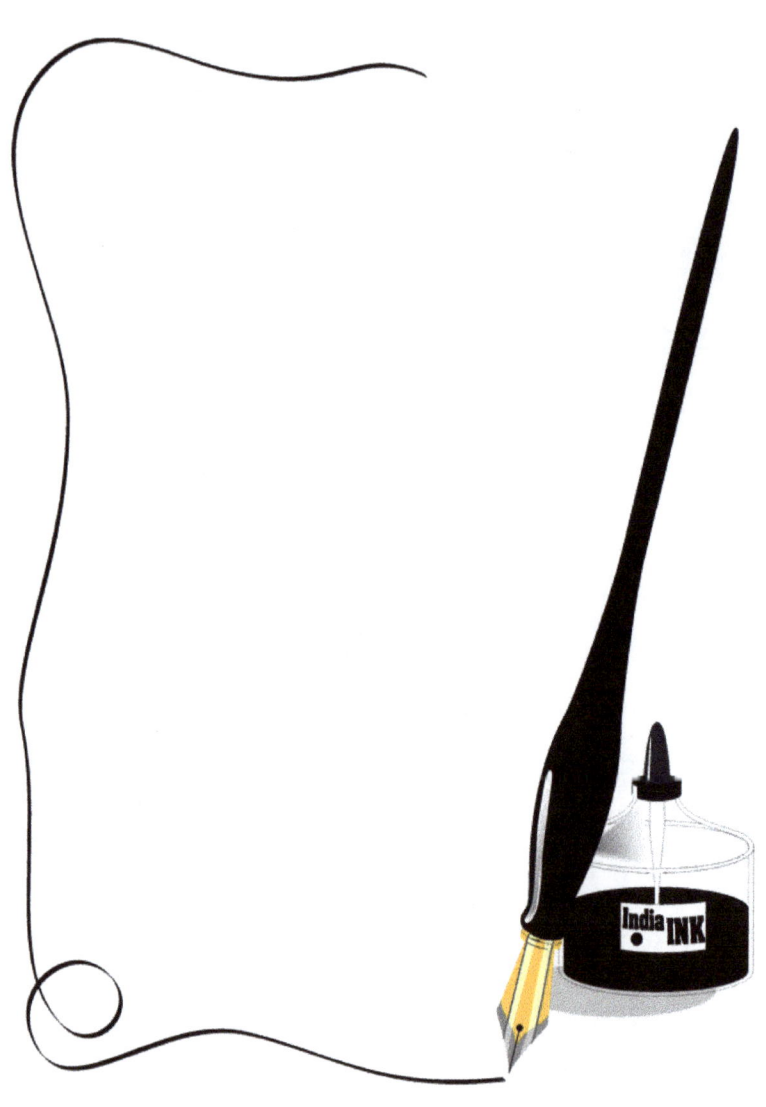

Contemplations ... *to be or not to be*

A Plea for Our Humanity

We may disagree on many issues. We may stand on opposite sides of the many lines drawn in the sand. Our politics may differ as well as our religious beliefs. What remains common with us all is so much bigger than the petty nuances found amongst us. The common bond is significant in that we are all human and we all are on the same Global Ship whether we like it or not. For far too long, we have allowed these differences to cause an unnecessary rife between us, when we all ultimately have the same goal . . . Peace, Love and Happiness. There is none amongst us in our right minds that truly wishes to suffer, yet we, many times, are the cause of not only the suffering of our own personal selves, but that of our fellow Human Family members.

We live in this world of turmoil that is slowly becoming more infested with bias, bigotry, greed, power mongering, climate disruption, war, homelessness, famine, pollution and disease, to name a few. We can, yes, CAN re-erect, re-invent, re-create the conditions that are suitable to all the inhabitants that occupy this "home" planet of ours. Contrary to some beliefs and deceits fed to the people, it never was about available resources. What we lack, we have the ability to improvise and make due. Such is the spirit of mankind, and womankind too. It is time for us to awaken, and by any means necessary, to come to the realization that selfish and self-serving interests have become outdated. Our world is at risk, for we trusted in the few to care for the many . . . and they have failed us tremendously.

We have an individual capability to meet all the challenges before us. Collectively, we are invincible. Now is the time for all good men and women to stand erect and let their voices speak out loudly for the change we all desire in our hearts. We can no longer use the excuses of fear and our lack of able-ness, for we all were endowed with a power that exceeds our finite understanding. It is time for the awakening of our divinity that we may recognize without the shadow of a doubt who we are, what we may become and where we are going as a Race of People on the Planet Earth. The choice is ours to make. Our hearts are much bigger and have a greater capacity to love and accept one and other than we can even begin to fathom! Let Love rule the days of our lives. Let a new day, a new reality be birthed within each of us.

Let us listen again to the music and learn once again to dance together. There is a wellspring of hope within each of our souls that has never been, can never be defeated. So, let us open the gates, lose the chains and become what we were created to be . . . gloriously divine . . . again!

Contemplations ... *to be or not to be*

A Poem in the Making

I want to be lyrical.
I want to be well-versed
In the use of a language
That is uplifting,
Informative,
And experiential.

I, at times, wish to rhyme.
Other times, not.

Sometimes there is a magic
Hidden in the subterfuge
Of chaos and discordance.

I want to transport my readers,
My observers
Into a place, a space
Within themselves
Where a common resonance
Is found between us.

I want to heighten our sensitivities
To the fact that
Though we are the building blocks
Of this world, this existence,
And the world remain
Bigger than us.

I want to espouse such things,
Such thoughts,

william s. peters, sr.

Such emotions
That inspire each of us,
Myself included,
To expand, to expand, to expand.

I want to invoke thoughtfulness and smiles,
Unmitigated laughter and love,
Contemplation, consideration and compassion.

I want to weave and offer
A cloak of humility
That we all can wear.

I am searching
For a humanity
That does not falter
When the Sun goes down,
Or when shadows and darkness
Creep stealthily into our
Sphere of influence.

I want to get to intimately know you,
And you, I . . . the lesser,
And the potential
Of what we collectively
Can become.

These things are possible. Truly!
For I have read the verse and lyrics
Of others, and
I am beyond measure
AMAZED.

Contemplations ... *to be or not to be*

And I sincerely believe
That not only I,
But we all
Are simply
A poem in the making.

Isn't that just magnificently grand?

william s. peters, sr.

For the People
Dedicated to all those who suffer the ways of our world

It is professed in the west
That government
Is 'for the people',
'By the people' . . .
But . . . is it really?

Truth be told,
We are fooled
Into being ruled
By the propaganda
Of the news agency
By Hollywood,
Social Media
And our schools . . .
What exactly is 'higher education'?
. . .
All of these
Are but tools
Of the elite class
And their 'elected/selected'
Minions we call politicians
To make decisions,
Counter to the will
Of the masses.

Wars, apartheid,
Economic sanctions
And other machinations
For the nations
Who do not conform

Contemplations ... *to be or not to be*

To the directed norm
Are the methodologies
Utilized
To make them realize
That 'size' matters
In matters of Statesmanship,
And whatever other bullshit
Being professed
By he who carries
The big stick.

Even though the 'people' tire
Of the unnecessary atrocities
That unnecessarily plague
'We the people',
What are we left with
To enact change?

People in steeples
Praying on their knees
At the altars of
Frustration and hope,
Protests and petitions
Hardly affect the positions
Of those who supply
Arms and munitions
To further perpetuate
The manufactured hate
That coddles the fate
Of us all.

If all the soldiers
Would just lay down their guns,
Where would the fun be

william s. peters, sr.

For those who like to kill
For the sake of killing,
Because life is but a statistic
In their bombastic evaluations
Of how to get more
More, more, more?

We stand by amused,
Confused,
Our emotions and opinions
Manipulated and used
To justify the evil
Being done by 'us'
Upon 'us',
While violating
The sacred trust
Of being human.

Do we do this 'for the people'?
Which people?
Or do we succumb
To the greed merchants
And warmongers
And their demonic ways?

'For the people'?
. . .
Hah!!!

Contemplations ... *to be or not to be*

You Can't Drink the Ocean

When swimming in the deep
And the tides of life overcome you,
Keep your calm and remember
'You can't drink the ocean'.

Keep your mouth shut
Below the surface,
And breathe in only
When your head
Is above the waters.

Don't fight the situation,
For you will tire
Before the ocean does.
As I said,
Stay calm and remember
'You can't drink the ocean'.

Meandering

Everything
Has its time,
Its place,
Its beginning,
Its end.

We meander through life,
And the lives of others,
As they do ours.

At times, we linger;
Sometimes, not long enough,
And at other times,
Than we should.
A tad bit longer

We hold on to things
We shouldn't have,
And let go sometimes
Sooner than we should;
But there are times
When we are rewarded
For getting it
Just right.

We think too long and hard,
And then there are times
We think too little,
Especially about ourselves.

We spend significant portions

Contemplations ... *to be or not to be*

Of our lives
Seeking meaning,
Reason and understanding,
Only to take a resolute stance
To stay stuck where we are
Or to move on . . .
Still seeking
Meaning, reason and understanding.

Who knows the way,
The path
Their life must take
To become fulfilled?
And . . . are we ever?

I look back on the years behind me.
Of course,
I could have taken
The road to the left,
Or the one to the right,
Instead of creating my own way;
Or, I could have retraced my steps
To the beginning
And started all over again.
However,
Would I be here,
Right here,
In this collection of moments
To reflect on
My own meandering,
And write poetry about it?

william s. peters, sr.

A Letter from Joy

Dear Dad,

How are you? I hope this brief note finds you in the highest of spirits. As you know Dad, I am rather a private spirit myself. I am writing to you, for, lately, I have had a penchant to be more outgoing. Yes, I do have my small circle of beloved friends, but something just does not feel complete within. Perhaps it is the coming of Spring and her family of Color and Song that entices me as well to come out and play more often. I just want to dance and sing as well in every heart I can touch. You should know this feeling well. Father, I wanted to ask you, though I do know you are completely against spells that enchant men to go against their will . . . however, could you just . . . give me a little one so I can once again feel the freedom of every heart embracing me in love and freedom to express their deepest inner bliss to one and all? Please, Dad . . . just one small Magic Charm?

Thank you, Dad, for your consideration . . .

Your Beloved Muse

Joy

Answer

My beloved and dear daughter of life,

Joy, why do you always come to me . . .?

Contemplations ... *to be or not to be*

Going to the Light

It was 3 o'clock in the morning, but the people did not know what time it was, because they could not tell time. They were chronologically illiterate.

Like most of us, we do not recognize, nor understand just how dire the circumstances are that we face as a humanity or inhabitants on this planet. We have already slept past the 11th hour.

This is not necessarily about global warming, nor is it about the glut of resources being plundered by an elite demonic class of citizens who thoroughly believe that you, I, we are expendable inventory here solely to do their bidding. No, this little inane tirade of thought converted to words is about you, me, us, and our continual dumb-downed approach to our own lives. You see, when we are awake, conscious, balanced and vibrating and resonating in harmony with the tonal essence of life, we will begin to see a light-filled change; 1st in self, then in others and things about us.

We somehow have put aside our ability to act upon the issues that affect the well-being of ourselves, the planet and the quality of life, while deliberately deluding ourselves by embracing such things as devices, social media, videos and television as a Saviour for our Angst and ongoing human anxiety. We have become drunk by the amount of 'likes', comments, shares, etc. we receive or share. SEE ME! I AM RELEVANT ... aren't I?

We shamefully have built gasoline-infused cotton houses of esteem that wait for that one spark to set aflame all that we are, all that we falsely embody, leaving us semi-obliterated by our unsecured insecurities. In the meantime, they are building spaceships for Mars, or is this too another ruse to milk the honey from the unpollinated flower with the use of selective political honeybees? Oh, to hell with it all! I have to take another selfie and post it. We will talk later . . . I promise!

Contemplations ... *to be or not to be*

A House on Fire

This is my home.
It was the home of my ancestors,
And yours as well.

What will our children
And our children's children,
Ad infinitum,
Inherit?

Greed, the avarice
And covetous postures
Have put it all
In danger of an ominous change
Or destruction,
And our silence condoned
This coming end.

. . .

But it does not have to be that way,
Does it?

Yes, there are still
Beautiful sunsets and sunrises,
Flowers, trees, birds
And butterflies.

We also have the mountains,
The skies
And the valleys

william s. peters, sr.

And our tremendously-at-risk
Streams and rivers, seas and oceans,
Not to mention
The air we MUST breathe
That we may live . . .

But live how?
The house is on fire!

Contemplations ... *to be or not to be*

Self

There was a time when I was not happy with 'My Self'.
So, I had a long, hard look at 'My Self'.
I decided I needed to change 'My Self'.
Most importantly, the image of 'My Self';
Especially the image I had of 'My Self'.
So, I began the self-improvement of 'My Self'
So that I could be happy with 'My Self'.

As I dug deeper within 'My Self',
I really started to find 'My Self'.
When I really began to discover 'My Self',
I realized that it was quite difficult to change 'My Self'.
Oh, for a little while, I fooled 'My Self'
Into Believing I was someone other than 'My Self'.
Then I realized I had to deal with 'My Self'.
So, I began to acknowledge 'My Self'.
Then came the realization of 'My Self'.
Then I accepted 'My Self'.
I even came to like 'My Self'
Because I was stuck with 'My Self',
Because I was blessed with 'My Self',
Because I was encouraged by 'My Self',
Because I was loved by 'My Self'.

In the discovery of 'My Self',
I really found 'My Self'.
My True Self within 'My Self',
The True Love of 'My Self'
Resided in HIM.

william s. peters, sr.

Crossing Au Naturel

We lose our parents.
Then we lose each other.
I pray my children
Go not before me,
And wait
For my journey to end.

Our grandparents
Have departed
So many years before,
And it has become
Increasingly difficult
To recall the Visions
Of their presence . . .
But the feelings remain.

Aunts, uncles, cousins and friends
Like leaves in the autumn
Drop to their resting place
One by one
. . .
Sometimes aided
By a strong wind,
A pouring rain
Or perhaps fatigue.
Or perhaps,
It was just their time.

When I look back
Over my shoulder
At what lies behind me,

Contemplations ... *to be or not to be*

I am aware
Of the words . . .
The words I spoke
And those I did not,
Or could not,
For I was busy and preoccupied.
Doing things,
Or doing much of nothing.

So, now I find myself
Relegated to writing poems,
Some contemplative,
Some reflective,
Some infused with my sorrows,
My pains,
My joys,
My hopes,
And a myriad upon myriad
Of dispositions
I wish to revisit,
And those I never had a chance,
Or never took the time
To experience.

But considering how I was reared up,
The thing more important
Than the cast-aside dreams,
The achievements and failures
Is the hope,
The hope that
I will see you all once again
For that eternal embrace.

william s. peters, sr.

I Am a Book

I am a book
That is being written,
That shall never be finished.

I am a story being told,
Being made up
As I go along.

There are words
That may have defined me,
My journey of the past.
New words
Will come to be
To define me
And what lies before and after.

I am a book
With words of indefinable treasure
That measure naught
But imagination.

I, as you are, am filled
With intrigue
For those who wish to inspect
But a little bit closer.

Tell me who you are,
And perhaps that will assist me
In finding me
In the definitions
Of life.

Contemplations ... *to be or not to be*

Let us sit, commune and read together
That we may come to know each other
A bit more
Before we shelve the book
That yet requires
A bit of review
And possible editing.

I am a book.

william s. peters, sr.

A World of Seekers

We all are seeking something. If we look around us, we can see that in each soul. Some are seeking Peace . . . some Love . . . some Acceptance . . . some Joy . . . some Understanding . . . some Wisdom . . . some Riches . . . some, just Abundance . . . some (more these days) are just seeking the basics of life such as food and shelter. The fact is, everyone, or at least the vast majority of us, are seeking. I guess you can say that we live in "a world of seekers".

The funny thing about this subject matter, when it came upon my wave of being, I first began to seek its significance and whether it would become a worthy topic to share. I, at that point, was seeking a "Pre Approval" of sorts. As we mitigate through these times of challenging such things within and without our "Self" . . . such things as Reality, Truth, Knowledge, Spirituality, God, Man and Consciousness, we might feel compelled to elect a path that most comfortably fits our own perspectives. We say that we are seeking, but just what is we are after . . . Confirmation or Discovery? Sorry for asking such a challenging question, but at some time, we must face our "Truest" of the Self in the mirror of our own Soul . . . not that of others. Perhaps these two seemingly incongruous attributes are somewhat symbiotic. Many seek within from a "Subjective" point of perspective and many of us are "Objective". I ask, where is the line that separates the two aspects of vision and focus of that which we desire, or quest for? Does not that which originates from our need for fulfillment (subjective) transmute itself to the objective?

Many times in these "times", we will hear people, myself included, speak of "BE"ing . . . and such things as "Here and Now"! Does the "Here and Now" change that we should

Contemplations ... *to be or not to be*

remove our "Self" from "BE"ing? Is all of what we know and seemingly understand governed by the rule we so innocently embrace such as "Time and Space"? It came to me in writing this last sentence that all that I have outside of these temporal parameters is my "Intent" . . . that alone permeates beyond my "BE"ing yet I am one with it! Yes, and there are times when I disconnect from "Intent" and become subject to these governing laws of Empiracy (a new word according to Dictionary.com, aka Empiric World).

Now, this article, really has no profound thing or subject to convey to you, save that you are the "Wonder of Creation". My only motive was but to share these reflections of "BE"ing with you that perhaps in your humble contemplations you embrace Discovery of the Divine and the majestic aspects Within and Without, and let the seeking by way of "Objectivity rest a bit.

Namaste'

Bill
"Seeker"

william s. peters, sr.

I Believe

In my daily encounters, I am asked many times, "how are you?" My reply is generically the same each time . . . "I am fine. I am alive, and that is a good start, considering the alternative . . . the rest is attitude".

Personally, I am a believer. What sense would life at all make if one did not have any beliefs in such things as Love, Hope, Dreams and Possibilities? This does not say that I am 'gung-ho' or diligent in pursuing the manifestation of these ideological virtues, but it does exemplify my core self and the direction my soul tends to wander towards.

The first step in bringing to fruition a more serene, peaceful, fulfilling and pleasant life experience lies within each of ourselves individually. This axis of self-empowerment is our attitude and our approach to what lies before us. Our attitude is something that is autonomous and completely in our control. Sure, there may be many outside influences, situations, circumstances, things and people who seem to embody the antithesis of our peace and power, but that only certifies that we have more ability to avert and deflect these energies that challenge, assail and attack us whether directly, indirectly, boldly or subtlety. We each are magnificent exponential souls with unlimited abilities to expand, grow and become even more powerful.

In conclusion, I say: If you wake up in the morning, you have a distinct advantage over all those who did not. The rest of your day is all about the attitude with which you approach it. If you think that you are a winner, you are! Conversely, if you think that you are a loser . . . you are! The choice is yours. Be very mindful of your energies and the '-tudes' in your life; that is, attitude, latitude, longitude, altitude,

Contemplations ... *to be or not to be*

platitude, solitude, aptitude, finitude, quietude, habitude, and so on. As they say, "attitude yields altitude".
I am a believer. What about you ?

william s. peters, sr.

A Poem I Wrote Today

I am obsessed
With verse
And rhymes and words
From the sane
To the absurd,
And back again.

So, here I am.
I sit upon this step,
Apart . . .
No friend
To be with, except in memory,
And in my heart.

There are many things
I could choose
To write about.
Or, I could just write
Until all the silly frivolous things
Leak out
Into the words I exact
Into this electronic device.

The metaphor we use
Of paper and pen or pencil
Is truly overused,
But what else can we say?
All we can do, and have done,
Was surrender our lives
To the 'age of electronics'.
Sadly so!

Contemplations ... *to be or not to be*

Please forgive me
As I ramble on
About things known
And need not be known . . .

. . .

But excuse me please!
I am trying to write a poem,
And I do need to say
Something, don't I?

. . .

Otherwise,
What is the use
Or purpose
To laud my 'self'
And speak about
A poem I wrote today?

william s. peters, sr.

My Heart Throbs

I have an affinity
For those
Whose hearts
Are bigger than their thoughts.

Though, some hearts
Are filled with shadows
And darkness,
But there is hope.
For, as long as that heart beats,
There is an inextinguishable light
That fights
To be seen.

I have learned
To trust more
In the possibilities
Than this illusory
Malleable reality
That changes
More than the weather.

Speaking of change . . .

I may not be here,
But I refuse to
Let go of this
Rope of hope
That binds and ties
My dreams for

Contemplations ... *to be or not to be*

My children,
Your children,
Humanity
To the future.

My heart throbs
As it has been
For many a year,
Filling my universe,
Your universe
With an immutable love
For what may be.

Maybe someday,
All of our hearts
Will give way to the day
When we shed the veils
That obscure
Our best selves.

Yes,
My heart throbs
With a belief
That this will
Come to be.

william s. peters, sr.

All Because of Freshly Cut Grass

Freshly Cut Grass . . .
The Smell of Fresh Dirt . . .
Looks Like Rain . . .

And . . . the pain of the "sane" people still taps lightly at their inane consciousness to remind them they are still stuck here, in this "fuck you"-here as the vibration of the expressions of life . . . SMDH . . . again.

It was Saturday again. Time for folks to get about the chores. Doors opening and closing, "SLAMMING", people hosing down their cars and flower gardens. Children have not started making noise quite yet, but you can bet your seditious ass they will very soon . . . sometime before noon. But I could hear those damn lawnmowers . . . my God, it is not even 8 o'clock yet! Don't those people have any decency? Where is my clemency from this purgatorious awakenings to another Saturday Hell . . . do tell!

In the meantime, a couple of blocks over to the slight South, the Angels were gathering firewood . . . lots of it. There was to be a "Stake Party" later this evening after the Sun went down. They, along with the approval of the Over-Lourdes, had selected 3 souls for their sacrificial amusements tonight. The whole neighborhood was gleeful as they anticipated the coming martyrdom of their once embraced friends and family. I guess they were also somewhat relieved that their straw was not the short one again. Many of them had experienced this way before only to be recycled in that ever-confluent path of reincarnation. This was the new age salvation. Die . . . ascend and be born again. Some peoples had not quite got the sequence down to rote, and attempted

Contemplations ... *to be or not to be*

to convince themselves they were born again even before they died. Another SMDH moment for me.

I lay in the bed looking up at the ceiling and the dancing Pixies of Light that tried to camouflage themselves in the juxtapositions of light and dark, but I could see them clearly, for I was endowed with a sight. It must have been a mistake. I noticed in my last cycle; things were a bit different. I could see things I later learned to keep to myself. Very few understood, or they feared acknowledging perhaps that they could see strange things too. Either way, I was not going to live my life completely in denial. I had bridges to burn this time around. Perhaps that would assist me with my convictions of heart as I attempt to keep the drones at bay.

They say, "This is the Day the Lorde has made" . . . not quite grasping the import of this simple edict of one's base belief systems, I question in my ignorance, "Which Lorde do you speak of?" In my simple observations, I have seen many colluded expressions of a delusional reverence, exercised as a truth to be digested by the masses. Here we go, another SMDH moment. Seems to be plenty of that going around these days.

In the meantime, on the other side of this finite Galaxy, there are other symbiotic dimensions being created and explored by the innocent seekers of a verifiable truth. To no avail. We being naught but projective creators are free to live that which we choose. Sometimes I question that "Gift" of Free Will, for it came without instructions, guidelines or restraints. So, we are free to paint upon life's palette in any colors or shapes as we so wish. Yet, there are reproofs and rebuke-ments being manifested to balance our equations of desire that we must suffer along. Some of us have learned the gift of song that we may hopefully entice the Gods to be merciful in our Praise-Like offerings to their ears . . . sort of

william s. peters, sr.

how our Role Model Lucifer did when he occupied the position of Ministry of Music. Now, we all have garnered a new craft and skill-set as we seek to be appeased and unstrung from this diseased experiential journey. In the end, I wonder . . . yes, I wonder, and all I can seemingly come up with are these sorts of semi-epiphanic emanations of Shaking My Damn Head. It is not that I am thoroughly convinced we are damned, for I, too, feel a compellation and thirst for salvation . . . a hope that will deliver me out of this continual vortex where anguish and joys conspire with one another to make for some sort of lesson. This is one for the ages where the absence of time is a reflective illusion as well. Oh, by the way, did I allude earlier about something of "sane" people? Don't believe it! For all is still yet held in the delicate balance of Chaos; for, from that primal space, a God of the people was borne.

All because of freshly cut grass . . .

Freshly Cut Grass . . .
The Smell of Fresh Dirt . . .
Looks Like Rain . . .

Contemplations ... *to be or not to be*

The Quietude

It was a dark, damp

Silent twilight,

Except for the

Faint chirping of the crickets

Far away,

And the noisy one

That lived somewhere

In our house.

william s. peters, sr.

Small Things

I was sitting outside
In the stillness of the night,
Smoking a cigarette,
Listening . . .
And all I could hear
Was this thumping,
Bmp bmp bmp
Bmp bmp bmp
Bmp bmp bmp
. . . and the crickets.

Sometimes in life,
Mostly by accident,
Rarely by intent,
We get to reverently appreciate
Those small things,
That thumping sound . . .
Bmp bmp bmp
Bmp bmp bmp
Bmp bmp bmp . . .
The beating of my heart
. . . and the crickets.

Contemplations . . . *to be or not to be*

Gratefulness

If we are honest with ourselves, we all must admit, there are things in our lives that we have and still take for granted. There are times past that were challenging, warm, memorable or spectacular that we have callously or indifferently relegated to the halls of memory . . . and somehow, we are okay with that. There are people who have passed through our lives, who had an indelible impact on who we are, our character, our life paths, and we are okay with going about our lives on a daily basis with no heart-felt or soul-filled remembrances of their significance. There are situations, people in our lives this day, today, that we do not make the time for a simple 'hello' or 'I love you'. There is so much more we can do to enhance our 'life experiences' to be that much more grander, colorful and meaningful than what they are. Additionally, we have the ability to do so for others.

We are an integral part of a wonderfully divine, unknown magical creation. We may not understand much about the whys, or how it all began, or what the purpose is, or where it all ends, but we do have the power to effectuate a change in the 'how' we walk through this garden of abundant potentialities. Let us not take any of this for granted.

If I have been able to stir you, your soul, your heart in any way this day, I wish to simply leave you with this: I reiterate, We are an integral part of a wonderfully divine, unknown magical creation. So, consider what your personal perspectives are on these words, and may you find a reason to celebrate your gratefulness for this life we have been afforded and touch someone with a loving compassion that re-energizes their soul, their beliefs in humanity and that of our own . . . simply because you, I, we can.

william s. peters, sr.

And I Breathe

Have I lived nobly?
Not always.
Am I doing so now?
The best I can do is try.

All too often,
We put aside,
Or forget
That which is important
In our little lives.

We oft' falsely
Inflate ourselves
To be more than what we are,
What is but a
Self-Delusion.

We are dependant upon
Illusory things
That we may have something
To which
We affix our values.

We say that we are thoughtful,
But that by definition
Is quite different than
Thinking.

We say that we care,
That we are considerate,

Contemplations ... *to be or not to be*

But even that premise
Is subject to
The tentacles of 'convenience'.

Love unequivocally?
That begins within,
But we spend far too much time
Chastising the 'Self',
Instead of forgiving
And embracing our
Misgivings and frailties
With compassion and understanding . . .
So, how does,
How can one
Truly love another?

When I breathe,
I am inspired
To exhale that
I may breathe again
And feed this machine
Of many needs,
. . . More than I am aware of.

In my solitude,
I sometimes get lucky
And touch my breath
With observance,
Hoping that perhaps I
Will discover something
Which is cherishable
Deep within my shallowness

william s. peters, sr.

That is worthy of
My continual and staid
Gratitude.

Oft times, I ponder such things
As 'Wisdom', an elusive anomaly,
But each time
I contemplate such things,

I realize my
Utter foolishness.

In the end-game,
(And it is a game),
The forces of existence
Relegate my ambitious self
To an abyss
Where silence and stillness abides,
And all that I am
Is but one breath away
From the next one,
And the next one
Ad infinitum . . . ?
. . .
Until they are no more . . .
Yet . . . still
I breathe.

Contemplations ... *to be or not to be*

Loved

A tender caress
Across my cheek,
A simple kiss upon my lips,
A few soft whispered words
In my ear,
The intimacy of the look
Deep in her eyes . . .
All conveyed to me
That I was uniquely loved.

Her touch was engaging.
Her kiss was inebriating.
Her words were captivating.
Her eyes were mesmerizing.
I belonged to her,
And she knew it.

william s. peters, sr.

An Interview with Death

Today, I was embracing my ever-present wonder, hoping to achieve a deeper and more profound understanding of life. So, I decided I needed to do an interview with Death. I made the call, and surprisingly, He, Death, answered the call personally and consented to this candid interview. This is a "LIVE" transcript of our "Sit Down".

Inner Child: Good morning, Death. How are you? Welcome . . . no! Wait a minute, I take that back.

Death: (chuckles) You are like most people. No one welcomes me . . . well, very few do.

Inner Child: Why do you think that is?

Death: (chuckles again) FEAR. Most people fear me.

Inner Child: (chuckles) True . . . but tell me why from your perspective.

Death: Beats me. It really does not make sense on a Truth Level or Cosmic Level. I am but a part of the natural evolution of things. I am inevitable for all living things. 'Change' is my surname.

Inner Child: Tell me, when you come to visit and take people away, where do you take them? Secondly, what is there to be afraid of?

Death: I take them Home . . . Home to where their souls have been aching for . . . that place of Peace. But there are many faces of me.

Contemplations ... *to be or not to be*

Inner Child: What do you mean?

Death: Well, there is Physical Death which is what most people fear. There is also Intellectual and Spiritual Death. Most people these days are on their way to dying in both of those realms in this expression of their existence. You can look at it this way . . . when I come and take them away, I am actually serving their requests to be unburdened by the circumstances they create. I am but a servant . . . just as all other aspects of expression of the Divine.

Inner Child: WOW! Really? I never looked at it that way.

Death: (quips) Because you, like most, are not looking . . . you are enduring and focused on survival instead of living.

Inner Child: So, back to Fear . . . tell me more about it.

Death: Fear is but a shadow you create to mask your own Light of Consciousness. I never did understand why you animals do so. Forgive me, for all animates have a survival instinct which somehow transmutes into Fear.

Inner Child: Why is that?

Death: Because you do not remember!

Inner Child: Remember what?

Death: That you are eternal Souls, and therein lies the ultimate truth. There is no such thing as Death.

Inner Child: So, you are telling me that you are a figment of my imagination?

Death: Close . . . but you, being the Co-Creator of your Temporal Reality, cosign to my existence, when in truth, I am like an Elevator, a Taxi Cab or an Escalator . . . I serve in the 'Soul-Level' of the "Transportation" industry.

Inner Child: (chuckles)

Death: I hope you get it.

Inner Child: I think I am . . . I kind of always felt that I was going to live forever.

Death: (chuckles) . . . Another Truth! There is no 'Forever'! There is just "IS-ness".

Inner Child: Wait a minute . . .

Death: (chuckles)

Inner Child: I am going to have to think on that . . .

Death: Don't over-think it like you do everything else. These are principles that are a bit beyond your ability to embrace them.

Inner Child: Duuuuhhhhhh . . . OK . . . I am speechless.

Death: I understand.

Inner Child: So, in closing, are there any parting words you would like to leave for the Listening and Reading audience?

Death: Yes, I most certainly would. You are here for an experience of a different vibration of what Life can be. Do not focus on me and what I am or appear to be. Let go of your fears and live your life. There will come a time in the

Contemplations ... *to be or not to be*

Karmic Classroom when you will be tested on the lessons you are being given in this manifestation. You have 'Free Will' to seek these lessons out and evolve to the next stage, so to speak. By focusing on what I am or appear to be, you cloud your 'Light Consciousness' as I said before. Focus on Life, for in truth you are an expression of Life and the Creator of Life. If you want to consciously conquer Death, then LIVE!!!

Inner Child: Death, I now truly would like to thank you for this opportunity to speak with you and for sharing these insights with us all. Blessings.

Death: I thank you as well. I will see you all soon (snickers).

Summary: In the end, when you consider how you will transition, what is important is how you live, what you carry with you and what resonance you leave behind. Did you leave your footprints in the 'Garden of Life' because you lived so prolifically with Love, Compassion, Understanding, Acceptance, Dreams and Wonder, or did you cower in the shadows of your greater expression of self?

In closing, I would like to thank you all for being here with us today.

Pondering

Off in the distant yonder

Where the clouds kissed the Earth,

I realized with an absoluteness

That everything is possible.

Contemplations ... *to be or not to be*

I Just Smile

Many are the things
I do not know.
Many things, I believe
I know.
So, what actually is the truth?
What is it I do know?

As I sometimes cruise,
Sometimes labor,
Sometimes just move
Through my life,
Sometimes inebriated
By my own doing,
Sometimes blindly disconnected,
Unaware and unresponsive,
I sometimes realize
That I do not realize
The impact I have
Or do not have
On the path I walk.
But we walk anyway . . .
Don't we?

In truth,
That is not an absolute.
For, sometimes
I am devoid of movement
As I lazily sit and watch
The parade
That passes before me . . .

william s. peters, sr.

And of course,
There are times when I run
Anxiously with anticipation
Towards the unknown.

Sometimes, in my quietude,
I am content to
Just be quiet,
While ignoring the subterfuge
That vies for my attention
And participation
In the useless 'tomfoolery'
That achieves naught.
. . .
I just smile.

Contemplations ... *to be or not to be*

As a Writer

As a writer, poet, humanitarian, and activist, I believe the goal of any conscious wordsmith is not to collect the 'likes', comments and certificates we display so proudly on social media; all of these things are wonderful, and it does feel good when our vanity is caressed. But . . . no, the ultimate objective is for our words to be read and perhaps understood.

I have been directly involved in the literary industry since 1966 through my own thoughts and subsequent written expressions. The primary reason as to why I took so eagerly to writing was simply because I found it much more fulfilling to be able to express my thoughts without interruption by way of the pen, as opposed to attempting to convey my ideas and developing theosophies through discussion.

william s. peters, sr.

Waiting

Being a poet,
I always said
That wherever you look,
There is a poem waiting
To be discovered,
Uncovered
And given . . .
Be it a passing
Thought, a verb or a noun
The ringmaster or the lion
The juggler, the clown.
In the city of lights
Or a rural town,
The smile of a child
Or a distasteful frown.

The inside out
Or upside down,
The Jester of court
Or the wearer of a crown . . .
No matter the color,
Red, white, black or brown,
Deep in the silence
Or some noisy sound.

In the darkness or light,
For the lost or the found,
The one who is free
And the one who is bound,
For the loose and tight

Contemplations ... *to be or not to be*

And the one unwound,
Whether one has wings to fly
Or is tethered to ground,
Triangles and squares
Or circles of round,
In sacrifice in plenty
Or a fleshly pound,
In the pits of hell
Or a mountainous mound,
Wherever one looks and listens,
There is that sound
Of that poem that is whispering,
Waiting to be found
And given
To the world.

william s. peters, sr.

A Rose Is Still a Rose

Mental tornadoes
And emotional hurricanes
Keep one off of their toes.

I attempt to stand upright
And not go every which way
When every single wind blows.

How the journey moves,
And where doth it end,
Who amongst us knows?

We howl at the moon,
Pray on our knees,
And cackle and caw like crows.

Like tears, streams and rivers
Run to the ocean,
So doth time flows.

Like obedient sheep
Who are taught but one way
We align ourselves in rows.

Over the cliff to our ruin,
To the blood-soaked valleys
Where yet still the flower grows.

With no angst to be found
On this sacred ground,
Yet forgiven are our foes.

Contemplations ... *to be or not to be*

With spirits now troubled
And once-pure thoughts stained,
We are still being led by our nose.

When we look in the mirror
Of our own delusions,
We strike the gamely pose.

We repeat to ourselves,
"I am OK, I am OK, I am OK"
In hope to escape our woes.

And through it all
As we continue to fall,
We realize ...
A rose is still a rose.

william s. peters, sr.

I Am but a Seed

A seed is planted
In the cold, dark dampness,
But it does not yield
To its conditions
Or the place where it has
Seemingly been abandoned.
. . .
No, it takes on the challenge,
For it knows
There is a life beyond
This . . .

It struggles against
That which would define it,
Its hull, the shell
That imprisons its promise,
And soon,
There is a break-unknown.

It is now redefining itself,
Metamorphosizing
As it begins to
Reach for an unknown,
And it looks back
From whence it came,
And realizes
It is a seed no more.

And as the journey continues,
The battle of challenges
Has just begun,
But it,
That which was once

Contemplations ... *to be or not to be*

But a seed,
Believes in possibilities
And magic.

Upon cresting the furrow,
It again transforms,
Growing earth-bound wings
That are kissed
By the sunlight,
The dew and the rains,
The gentle breezes and winds,
But it will not be daunted,
For it has discovered
The miracle of growth.

When it again looks back
From whence it came,
It assuredly realizes
That there is a sky above . . .
"Is that my limit?" it asks.

william s. peters, sr.

Good Morning!

It was a semi-foggy morning,

A bit chilly,

A bit too dense to see clearly,

But I could sense

The cut grasses

With the scent of wet hay

Assail my sense of smell . . .

And the "I" realized,

It is yet another

Good day to be alive.

Contemplations ... *to be or not to be*

Quick Enough

The solitude found
In a sustaining quietude
Ushers for an attitude of peace,
A place I am still
Trying to achieve.

I do believe
That if I can conceive it,
It is only a matter of time
When all the rhymes
Come together
For the better
Of myself,
And all mankind.

Being kind
Is not so difficult,
When we separate ourselves
From the cult-behaviors
Humans and hued-men embrace
To maintain the false face
We tightly hold onto,
To ratify
The false premise
Of self-importance
That ultimately leads
To our demise,
Regardless of past deeds
And all the seeds
We have sown.

Somehow,
I have always known

william s. peters, sr.

That as Bob Dillon says,
"The answer, my friend
Is blowing in the wind . . ."
So, why do we defend
These castles of sand
That ultimately will be
Overtaken and destroyed
By the tides of life
From which none may hide?

And . . . in the final analysis,
What we are left with
Is a gift,
If we simply make the shift
To understand
That the demands we perceive
Are but 'usions' . . .
Confusions,
Delusions, built-upon foundations
Of illusions . . .
Which yield unto our souls,
Our spirits,
Our hearts and our minds
Unhealable contusions.

So, while you are here,
Hear this:
You might as well
Enjoy the ride,
For it goes by fast,
And it is over
Quick enough.

Contemplations ... *to be or not to be*

Slaves

The true enslaved are those who hate. Their bondage is one of a soul-consuming anguish that they can never escape until they learn to let go and come to sincerely love that which they hate. Unfortunately, most are doomed to die with their pain intact.

william s. peters, sr.

A Sunday Morning Reflection

It was 1994
Or something like that,
A time so long ago.

I was younger then.
Well, of course, I was.
I even laughed
And so much more . . .
Of course I did,
For there were far fewer aches and pains.

I would like to think
I have become a bit wiser,
But that appears to be
In suspect,
For there are still small issues
That trouble me
That I cannot fully resolve.
So, I keep burying them
Deeper.

I still lament the loss of loved ones,
Some more so than others,
But though the pain is
Not quite as acute
As it used to be,
That shit still ain't cute.
So, once again,
I just dig the hole
A bit deeper
To bury my unresolved anguish.

Contemplations ... *to be or not to be*

Funny, amusing even,
How counselors and priests
And friends and charlatans
All espouse
That they know the way
To salvation . . .
Well, I listened often.
Why hell, I even followed a few,
Until we arrived at that cliff
Where they encouraged
Everyone except themselves
To jump off
. . .
Hah, I see myself as somewhat
Smarter than that!
. . .
Sometimes I consider
What did lie
At the bottom.
Is it any different
From the bottomless pits
Of my life
That I have frequented
From time to time
During this journey
We deem 'life'?

I often wonder
To what end
These personal examinations
Deliver my wayward soul unto.
. . .
I still find joy
In the laughter of children

william s. peters, sr.

And adults as well;
I still enjoy the seasonal grandeur
Of the Spring, Summer, Autumn and Winter,
But as I ingest these moments
Which create memories,
I ask,
Can I take them with me
To the next lifetime?

There is so much more
That I have to think about,
Surmise,
But far too often,
I close my eyes
To the possibilities
Of the evolution
That remain before me,
For I find myself sitting here,
Contemplating, judging
Without any finite commitment.

Am I wiser
Than I was in 1994?
Hah . . .
Why bother, I say.

That cliff still remains
For those who would consider
It as an alternative . . .
Me? I am satisfied
To sit here
And immerse myself in
A Sunday morning reflection.

Contemplations ... *to be or not to be*

The Fruits of Trust

Yes, 'Trust'
Is a wonderfully sweet
Ambrosiac quality
That all should experience
At least once
In their lives.
But . . . I say,
Why not vie to have it petition my Muses
To bring to me
The gift of words,
For I wanted to write about
'The Fruits of Trust'.

I am a witness
To the wonderful bounty and booty
Yielded unto those
Who are so blessed
To give
And to receive
This divine state of being.

In seeing the fruits
Of the seeds we plant,
Of 'Trust',
How can you not exclaim
To the world,
To all creation
Its sweetness?

'Trust' is an ingredient

william s. peters, sr.

Widely applied
In relationships
And encounters,
Those of love,
Those of friendship,
Those of some strangers
And some family members
As well.

I tell you,
It is better to have trust
Than not.
After all,
Who wants a life of wariness and weariness?
'Tis not a good way
To live
Throughout our lives.

As I said,
I can attest that
'The Fruits of Trust'
Are sweet.

Contemplations ... *to be or not to be*

If I Could . . .

Perhaps it is possible,
But no one has yet been able to do so.
If I could . . . write a poem
To end all wars,
Make all the soldiers
Lay down their arms,
Would I?
Yes to a stupid question.

If I could write a poem
That makes everyone look to see
The best in everyone
They know, see or meet,
Would I?
Yes, to another stupid question.

If I could write the poem
That would make all the 'Greed Merchants'
See the ludicrousness
Of their ways,
Would I?
Yes! Yet another stupid question.

If I could write the poem
That makes all
The religious and political zealots,
And those who harbor unreasonable bias
Toward their fellow man
Let go of their ways,

william s. peters, sr.

Would I?
Yes. You understand . . .
Another stupid question.

If I could
Find the means
To infuse my words
With a power
That evokes a change
For the better,
Would I?
. . . need I ask?

If I could but learn
To touch the hearts, minds, and souls
Of those who still take the time
To read . . .
Gee, how cool would that be!

There are so many things
I would do
If I could.

Perhaps it is possible,
But no one has yet been able to do so.
If I could . . .

I am trying.

Contemplations ... *to be or not to be*

Me and Thee

I have spoken your name
A thousand times,
But once was quite enough.
Since that very first time,
I somehow felt that
You belonged to me,
And I to you.

From thence,
That initiative moment
We have traveled and traversed
An unknown road,
Creating our own
Way to go,
Our own pathway
Together . . .
As One.
And 'One'
We shall always be
All ways.

There is something, some thing
That lives and breathes
Beyond the realm
Of what we call 'Love'.
There is something, some thing
That is vibrant and brilliant
That infects the soul
Of those who . . .
Those who . . .
. . .
The words I cannot speak,
But if you just happen

william s. peters, sr.

To get a peak,
You will definitely understand
My intent.

There is something inside me
That you have touched,
Of which I, in my naiveté
And ignorance,
Was circumspect
Of its existence,
But together we journeyed,
Together we wondered.
As we wandered,
We discovered a commonality
That 'lived to live'
Within each of us,
And we sat in the stillness,
The quietude,
And absorbed the aural magnificence
Of 'Presence' and its peace.

I am filled,
Yet I am empty.
I am joyful.
I am resolved.
I am traveling, moving
In a world of stillness
Where all things are budding,
Blossoming and blooming,
And yielding a fruit
For wayfarers
Such as I . . .
Wayfarer
Such as you,
   . . .

Contemplations ... *to be or not to be*

And the rewards
Of our journey
Are found along the way
For he who hungers,
And he who thirsts . . .
But I hunger, I thirst
No more.
For, I have you
Who satiates my needs.

Kiss me, my love!
Kiss me, kiss me,
And let me once again
Lose myself
In the euphoria of
Your touch,
Our connectedness.
Kiss me,
And let me lose myself
In you, and you in me.
Kiss me, and kiss me again!
For, my desire for thee
Is ever growing
For
Me and Thee.

william s. peters, sr.

Just an Ordinary Reflection

Not too long ago, we were at a family gathering at my brother Rodney's home. We had all just left a 'home-town' event . . . Chesilhurst Day. During our fun and camaraderie at Rodney's, he and my pseudo brother Cliff noticed that I was wearing suspenders. They began to laugh. It did not really move nor disturb me, for these suspenders I wear serve a much-needed and welcomed function of holding my trousers up.

As I reflected on the incident of their mirth and jovial prodding, I know with an undue certainty that it was all in love, and spawned by a few beers and the arrogance of youth. You see, there is about 17 years between my youngest brother and me. At the ripening age of 71, I can vaguely remember my parents and grandparents occupied this plane of ageism. I really thought they were old. Though I had love and appreciation for who they were, what they were and all that they contributed to life, especially that of mine own, my other family members and their community, I never saw myself at the place I am now.

What is the significance? Throughout my time on the 3rd rock from the Sun, I have witnessed the transition/transcendence of not only my loved ones such as soul-partners, parents, aunts, uncles, grandparents, cousins, but also of friends, acquaintances and associates. What I am left with in reflection is an overwhelming sense of gratitude. It is such an honor to see these days and nights. Though many are the challenges and issues one must confront, I still think it is better to be here to do so.

This morning as I thought about this seemingly small encounter with my conscious position, I felt compelled to

Contemplations ... *to be or not to be*

examine myself a bit more thoroughly and what meaning/message was attempting to garner my attention. It was simple: GRATITUDE. I then began to question, what exactly is gratitude? Is it the mere declaration of being thankful? Is it the character and posture of how one carries him or her self? Is it the actions of the individual, their contributions to life itself and that of others? What exactly is gratitude? How does one live and exude gratitude in all of their being . . . heartbeat, thoughts and breath? Is there a magic key to the magic room of whom each of us must discover and thus walk into? Is it a pool of liquid consciousness that beckons us to strip naked, devoid ourselves of the empirical-ness of this world, and jump in for a swim . . . drown even? What exactly is gratitude? Well, when I GOOGLED the word, this is what I came up with:

Grat·i·tude
/ˈgradəˌt(y)o͞od/ noun: gratitude

The quality of being thankful; readiness to show appreciation for and to return kindness.

What is the true meaning of gratitude? Gratitude is a positive emotion that involves being thankful and appreciative, and is associated with several mental and physical health benefits. When you experience gratitude, you feel grateful for something or someone in your life and respond with feelings of kindness, warmth, and other forms of generosity. According to the Department of Education at Berkeley, psychologists have determined that there is more to what gratitude is and represents:

"What are the three types of gratitude?" Some psychologists further categorize three types of gratitude: gratitude as an "affective trait" (one's overall tendency to have a grateful disposi-tion), a mood (daily fluctuations in overall grati-tude), and an emotion (a more temporary feeling of gratitude that one may feel after receiving a gift or a favor from someone).

What stood out for me in this declaration was the word 'temporary'. Personally, I want something more than the transient.

The Cambridge Dictionary spoke of 'thankfulness', specifically alluding to the type of thankfulness one has when one is given a gift. Now, as I see it, this is a bit complex. For me, in my compromised mind, to be thankful for the gifts one is given by others is one thing, but to be thankful for the gift of life, or should I more aptly say, the gift of this experience we call life? Well, that embodies something I believe is the journey we all are on; it truly is the discovery of our greater selves, our authentic selves, our atman (AKA the universal self), the 'self' and our 'non-self'. I truly believe, when we understand the yin and yang of it all—which include and encompass Life and Death; Light and Darkness; Saintliness and evilness and all other polarized positions of this experience—then, and only then may we embrace an appreciation of the true essence of gratitude.

This has been nothing, but everything to start this day of mine . . . it is just an ordinary reflection. I must thank my beloved brothers Rodney and Cliff for being the catalysts for me in this examination.

Contemplations ... *to be or not to be*

As the Brilliance Fades

We traverse the mountainous pathways,
We mitigate the valleys and the meadows,
We saunter along the sandy beaches,
We challenge the briar
And the uncharted wood,
Making a path for ourselves
As we journey and pray our way
Through life.

Yes, there is hope, of course,
And dreams as well
That encourage us to continue
To go forward
To the next day
With mild expectations
Of something more intriguing
Than our yesterdays.

We sail the seas and the oceans,
We swim in the lustrous lakes,
We stick our toes in the streams and brooks,
Trying to whet our spirits
With that missing wonder
We were once familiar with
In the days of our youth.

We turn over rocks,
Collect stones, pebbles and shells,
Chase butterflies and fireflies
And flee wasps, snakes and bees.

william s. peters, sr.

We sit
In each day's solitudes
To listen to
The chirping of the
Early morning birds,
The owls who hoot
In the evening-tide
Who orchestrate
Along with the crickets
To serenade us through the night.

We look to the horizon
In awe of the grandeur
Of the setting sun,
We anticipate the rising
Of the new days to come.

We justify in our hearts
And our minds
The medicinal tasks before us,
Along with the edible delicacies
Of our expectations.

We are a strange fruit,
Are we not?
Is not this
What normal looks like?

We labor much,
We exhaust ourselves at times,
So we have a seat
As the luminous aspects
Of the day
Begin to wane.

Contemplations ... *to be or not to be*

We reflect
On times past and beyond,
Circumspectively examine
The footprints behind us,
Along with the spirit-filled
Faces we encountered
Along the way.
. . .
The smiles, the frowns,
The exasperation, the wonder.

We reach back to visit
Once again
And again
All the things
Our eyes have seen,
Embracing the moments,
Cherishing the privilege
Of having had the opportunity.

Yes, a wonder it is
To again revisit the fullness
Of it all
As the brilliance fades.

william s. peters, sr.

The Journey

I found a poem today—
A solitary red autumn maple leaf,
Pretending to be a butterfly,
Fluttering in the gentle fall breeze,
Suspended in the cobwebs
I never got around
To brush away.

I can relate. Really!
For many times, I feel too
As if I am hanging
In a limbo,
Waiting for something . . .
A breeze, a wind
To free me from my entanglements
That I may experience fully
The next step
Of my finite journey.

Contemplations ... *to be or not to be*

I Dance

I do not recall
If I heard the music playing,
But I dance anyway.

In spite of the fears,
The doubts,
The anxieties,
The worries and troubles,
I dance.

In my joys,
In my sorrows,
In my wakefulness,
In my sleep,
I dance.

I dance
Because I am happy,
And in my sadness too.
When I dance,
My melancholy flees.

I dance in the darkness.
I dance in the light.
I dance to the sunrise.
I dance as the sun sets.
I dance to the moon.
I dance to the stars.
Yes, I dance.

I dance to the seen
And the unseen as well.
I dance to what is past.

william s. peters, sr.

I dance to what is to come.
I dance to the 'here'.
For, this is where I AM . . .
I dance.

I dance in the storms,
The rains and the winds
And the fair days as well.
I dance because my heart still beats.
I dance for each breath.
I dance.

I dance to escape,
I dance and I am captured.
I dance with abandon.
Yes, again, I dance.

I dance to the noise.
I dance within the silence.
I dance because I can.
I dance,
I dance,
I dance.

I dance for no reason,
I dance just because.
I dance,
I dance,
I dance . . .
Will you dance with me,
Please?

Any excuse,
Any reason,
Or lack thereof will do . . .
Let us dance!

Contemplations ... *to be or not to be*

The Magic

It was one of those days
That teeter-totters between
The waning summer
And the coming autumn.
Not too hot, not too cool . . .
Just right
For my temperament.

I feel a restlessness
That may be leftover
From a Spring season past.

I want to get out and explore
Once more
Before the grand tapestry
Of the changing colors
Of the leaves upon the trees
Once again introduces its majesty
That entices my soul
To reflect
As I consider the end season,
Winter
And what that time of the year evokes.

Perhaps I am getting a bit
Ahead of myself,
But it matters not,
For I have seen this show
Many times before . . .
But the magic still prevails.

Perspectives

One man shoveled pig shit for a living and cursed the day he was born. Another shoveled pig shit for a living and was happy and ecstatic, for he knew that the more pig shit he shoveled the more money he made to provide for his family. One man passed the pile of pig shit shoveled each day and cursed its existence. Another man deliberately went to the pile of pig shit each day to gather as much as he could that he may fertilize his garden.

The irony of this treatise is that all men ate from this garden the fruits and the vegetables as did their families.

Sometimes life will give you a pile of shit to work with. How you perceive it and what you do with it makes all the difference.

Contemplations ... *to be or not to be*

A Conundrum

I have struggled with Demons
And Angels alike,
As I have weighed myself
In the vast void
Of Life and Death.

I have sinned greatly,
And I have blessed as well,
Taking ownership
Of virtues and avarice
That never really belonged to me.

I have been an enemy
And an ally,
An adversary
And a comrade,
A cheerleader
And a hater,
A coach
And a subverter.

I have engaged in dreams of others,
And avidly embraced indifference,
Believing my stance
To be wholly holy.

I at one time loved and lived
By the credo of hypocrisy,
And convinced myself
That I was righteous.

william s. peters, sr.

There is a hole
In the middle of
All men's hearts
Where we can slip
And lose ourselves
As well as our
Presumptuous halos.

We curse our fate and our faith,
Espousing them to be the reason
Of our lack,
So we loquaciously embrace
Our self-doubt
While we decry our faults.

What is this thing we call 'soul'?
Is it ingestible, digestible
Or just another contestable point,
Along the axis of this
Malleable illusory reality?

My final analysis falls
Into the realm
Where all logic lends itself
To the immutable, commutable
But not refutable-ness
Where conundrums
Reign as reasonable-ness,
For there is naught else
That aptly contains our confusion

A conundrum . . .

Contemplations ... *to be or not to be*

Who Knows?

We arise each day
In an 'air', laden
With a dulled uncertainty
Of what the day before us may hold,
And how it all will unfold.

We have our rote-full routines,
Such as . . .
Have a visit to
The porcelain throne,
Wash our hands, our faces,
Shower, shave, brush our teeth,
Getting dressed,
And coffee, yes coffee . . .
Or juice if you prefer.

Perhaps today,
We will achieve some semblance
Of a reliable clarity
And discover that we have
All that we need . . .
Within,
Or perhaps today
Will be like most days
Where we become occupied
By task and duty
To put such things aside
On our 'wish list',
Or in our 'bucket' full
Of dreams
Titled 'Some Day'.

Who knows?

william s. peters, sr.

Perhaps some day,
We will get a glimpse
Of absoluteness
And the full magnitude
Of how powerful we are
To effectuate change . . .
Singularly and collectively.
Who knows?
. . .
We know, don't we?

We are empowered!!!

Contemplations ... *to be or not to be*

The Making of Jesus

You gave us a hypothetical construct
Which you fashioned in Nicaea,
All to garner a control
Over the minds of people.

For us who were born of the Motherland,
You stripped us of our heritage
Before you gave us a cross
With some eurocentric effigy,
Posturing as a sacrifice.

You allowed us to read
This thing you called
"A Bible",
And somehow,
We found solace
In the belief
Of the words it spoke
And in the coming salvation.

Lord knows,
We are long overdue,
Going back to the
Pre-Trans-Atlantic enslavement
Of people like me.

So, over the years,
We adopted and
We took your Jesus,
And hung pictures and crosses
In our homes

william s. peters, sr.

To further the imperialism
And colonization
Of our minds
Which our spirits
Hungrily acquiesced to.

We gathered, as instructed,
Of the false Sabbath,
Worshiped, danced and sung . . .
Trying to invoke that coming
You have been promising
For over 2,000 years
. . .
Coming soon, coming soon, coming soon . . .

In time,
We have built our own iconic images
Of 'Our Lord and Saviour'.
Why, we have even given Jesus
A promotion,
And we pray mostly
To the messenger
And not its source . . .
An oddity for sure!

Is our Creator
A White man,
A Black man
A Yellow man,
A Red man?
Is our creator made
In our image,
Are we, in His?

Contemplations ... *to be or not to be*

Is our Creator
A male, or
A woman,
Or is our Creator
Androgynous?
Or is our Creator
An energy beyond
Our simple and meager understanding?

In the meantime,
Back on Jesus' tip . . .
We have fashioned
This Jesus you gave us, Constantine
To now be bigger
Than life itself.
Odd, for the words of thus Jesus
Are clearly misunderstood,
Manipulated,
And fashioned into a modicum
Of convenience.

We have taken what you gave unto us,
Enhanced it
And romanced it.
We fell in love with
An anomaly
Of the making of man . . . damn!
I guess I am going to hell.
For . . . you know,
That truly,
Heaven and Hell
Are how you perceive
Them to be.

william s. peters, sr.

You see,
As they say,
You came to our Motherland
With your 'Bible'
Which you gave to us.
You then asked us
To close our eyes
And pray with you,
And we trustingly
And foolishly complied.
When the prayer was done,
We opened our eyes
To see that we had your 'Bibles'
To keep us in line,
But it was you
Who had our land.

This was lesson 101
Of how to colonize
The minds that you find
In your global explorations
Of discovery of lands,
Occupied by peoples
Who do not look like you.
And . . . if the missionaries and bibles
Do not work,
You revert
To your barbaric nature,
And massacre, slaughter and enslave
With your demonic inclinations.
But . . . wait,
The class that teaches
The rudimentary elements
Of colonialism

Contemplations ... *to be or not to be*

Is far from over,
For we still cling
To this Jesus
You gave to us
A long time ago . . .
Though
We have now
Re-colorized his stature

. . . . to be continued . . . .

The making of Jesus . . . .

Jesus now is BIG BUSINESS!!!!

william s. peters, sr.

Could Be . . .

It could be tomorrow.
It could be today.
It could be years from here
And miles away.

Perhaps it has already passed us by,
And perhaps it has not
But the ultimate question the soul asks is
"Will we remember what we forgot?"

From whence have you come
And what road do you travel?
The more life seems to come together,
The more it unravels.

Truth appears to be subjective.
Is that something one can stand on?
We click our heels and blink twice,
And voila, Truth be gone!

Is doubt, pain and fear a reality,
Or just another delusion
To remind ourselves that once again
We have succumbed to the illusion?

Are we the masters of our fate?
In what realm does this truth exist?
For, if this is the sum of our being-ness,
I demand that these variables desist.

Contemplations ... *to be or not to be*

I fool myself with such things,
Telling myself, I have false fortitude.
In the end, that too, my friend,
Are the misgivings of my transient attitude.

So, most times as I think on these things,
I take a deep breath and sigh,
And find myself right back where I started,
Simply asking the simple question: why?

The possibilities may be endless,
And the potentialities are vast.
That which possibly 'Could Be'
Was spawned in that forgotten past.

So, again . . .
Most times as I think on these things,
I take a deep breath and sigh,
And find myself right back where I started,
Simply asking the simple question: why?

Could be . . .

william s. peters, sr.

Sprung

Standing by on
The roadside of life,
I patiently await
The re-dawning
Of my favorite season.

I must keep my eyes open.
The gate to my spirit, unlocked,
Remains ever vigilant.
For, should I close my weary eyes,
I will find that
Spring has 'Sprung' . . .
Oh, what a travesty!

Imagine living a life
Where there is no fragrance
In your garden,
No pollinating bees
To collect the sweet nectar
We so embrace and cherish;
No butterflies for the children
To chase;
No chirping birds,
Budding and blooming flowers,
No immensely fair days,
No Spring showers to
Soothe our troubled hearts.

For some reason,
Though the summer is joyous,
The autumn is so colorful
And filled with promise
Of a bountiful harvest;

Contemplations ... *to be or not to be*

The winter provides
The time to enjoy
The delectable fruits
Of our previous toil, and
The much-needed respite
From our self-created
World of chaos and movement.
What would it all mean
Should we close our eyes
But for a bit
And awaken to realize that
Spring has 'Sprung'?

'BE'!

william s. peters, sr.

It's All Good

When you think about it,
All the ups and downs
And turnarounds,
The good, the bad,
The things and times you had
And lost
. . .
The costs we had to pay
May have been high,
But here we are,
Still standing
With less demanding,
Appreciating
Where we are.

I am here,
Filled with
An immeasurable gratitude
To be where I am.

I look back
At all the exciting things,
My soul singing its way
Through all my tears and joys.

The happiness, the pain
And all the inane insane
Personas I disguised as me . . .
Of course, this is long before
I could see

Contemplations ... *to be or not to be*

That life had so much more
To offer
Than my short-sightedness
Could comprehend,
But no matter,
I enjoyed myself
And I am blessed
With few regrets.
. . .
Are not regrets a heavy burden
To bear?

It's all good.

william s. peters, sr.

Acceptable

When the 'crazy' becomes normalized,
Does that give us the excuse
For our silence?

When the asylum is overrun
By those who occupy its purpose,
Should we turn our backs?

When do you lend a 'deaf ear'
To the propaganda and
The insane rhetoric
That continually assaults
Your desensitized peace?
. . .
When do we stand,
Mobilize and rage against,
Fight back
Against this demonic virus
Which/who gives not a damn
About humanity
And the innocent casualties
Lost in a war
They did not start,
Nor wanted?

What the hell does
"Acceptable" mean?

Contemplations ... *to be or not to be*

Those Days

I remember those days
When we ate fish
Every Friday
For dinner.

Hot dogs and baked beans
On Saturdays,
Because our cook
Took the day off,
Because Sunday
Was a big day
. . .
Roasted chicken, cornbread
And sometimes ham,
Collard greens,
Macaroni and cheese,
Potatoes or rice and
Kool-Aid.

Monday was a day of
Leftovers,
And Tuesdays and Wednesdays
Were sort of
Pot-luck days . . .
A lot of stewed beef
Over rice and
Kool-Aid
. . . .
She always wore an apron . . .
. . .
Lunch was
Peanut Butter and Jelly
Or Bologna and cheese,

william s. peters, sr.

Hand-sliced at home.

Breakfast was
Bacon and eggs,
Sometimes we got home-fried
Home fries
With sautéed onions.
. . .
Cold cereal was the treat
Back then . . .
Oh, how I loved "Corn Flakes"
There was no "Captain Crunch"
Or "Tony Tigers" in those days.
Mom, she loved those nasty
Bran Flakes and Shredded Wheat . . .
Stuff that made a boy like me
Choke.

I was a pre-teen
Before I went to a McDonalds.
There was not much of a choice
When it came to 'fast foods' . . .
Now, I get dizzy and confused,
Trying to figure out
What I have a taste for.

Those days
Of long ago,
Though I do not lament nor regret,
I do so miss . . .
Those days

Contemplations ... *to be or not to be*

Being Reflective

I look back at all the dreams I have chased; all the things I have hoped and wished for; all the different persons and characters I pined to be, and I realized that all of it was meant to be to deliver me to where I am . . . I AM. Isn't life amazing?

william s. peters, sr.

To Be or Not to Be

No/Yes . . .
I have not always listened
To the voices of authority,
Nor have I listened to the voices
Of my loving muses,
But I can declare this:
I have always listened
To the conflicting, unsure, circumspect
And sometimes resolute
Voices in my head.

All that I have done
In this journey we call 'life'
Is subject to judgment,
But who is qualified
To do so?
Why, not even I
Feel comfortable
Condoning or condemning
The actions of my past,
Or those now embraced
In the arms of my
Morrows.

What is to come
Remains a mystery,
Regardless of
My well-laid plans
Which I have labeled
As absolute certainties.

Contemplations ... *to be or not to be*

Isn't life a grand conundrum?
As they say,
We'd be damned if we do,
We'd be damned if we don't.
So, are we just damned?

Either way,
Life moves on,
Even in the face of death.

We all question
From time to time . . .
What is to come?
Or
What if?
. . .
I find it all quite amusing,
When I consider the impact
And the hand
That fate and destiny plays
In this card game of life.
. . .
Sometimes I have drawn
A full house,
Sometimes a pair or two.
Why, a couple of times,
I have drawn a crooked flush
And a few straights
Along the way.
. . .
I never cheated,
But I do long for
That sustainable Royal Flush
That solves and resolves

william s. peters, sr.

All the angst
I 've ever had.

I do realize
That experience is the teacher,
And many times in my contemplations
I conclude
It must be me, the student
Who studies too little,
And thinks too much.

In the end,
I ludicrously surrender
To the silence,
Listening for the voices
That speak not,
And my reflective 'self' subtly whispers
That it all is simply
To be or not to be.

Contemplations ... *to be or not to be*

Samsara

I am but another wanderer,
Seeking to find my way home,
But it seems like since
The beginning of time
And creation,
I am stuck in a loop
Watching eons, old reruns
Of movies.
I vaguely remember
Creating new perspectives
That alter the truth
Of it all.

I have seen many things
Of which most
Have been consciously forgotten,
But I do know
That the sub-consciousness
Of my existence
Has with due diligence
Recorded all the nuances
For my future reference
And potential use.

Each day,
I look forward
To the edibles of spirit,
And what shiny secrets
Cloak themselves
Beneath the surface,

william s. peters, sr.

Whispering to me
To pay attention
And observe the 'tells'
That may lead me
To yet another
Significant 'Kismet' moment
As they wander symbiotically
Through me,
As I do with life.

What is the purpose
Of this journey?

Though many profess
To know the answers,
How can one solution
Be a 'fit all' for all,
When the variables of life
Cannot be counted
In this lifetime?

Samsara, I say, Samsara
Is the best I can conjure,
And yet the questions
Continue to loom about
For those of us
Who are but
Wandering through.

Contemplations ... *to be or not to be*

Minor Distractions

There will always be
Things,
People,
Circumstances
Seeking to distract you
From fully engaging
In the essence of beauty.

They hang around,
Stand before you,
Whisper suggestively
Or scream, if it serves
Their purpose.

Why, even if you
Wish to look within,
You must navigate
Through the wilderness
That you may arrive at the door
That transforms the illusions
Into the reality
That everything about and around you
Possess, a mesmerizing charm,
Waiting for your soul
To embrace.

There are minor distractions
We too create,
Be it the 'putting off',
Errant thoughts,

william s. peters, sr.

Laziness and indifference,
Or just closing one's ears
And not hearing
The song of life
Playing a tune
Just for you.

What we deem to be
Life itself
Is also but a minor distraction
From that which is eternal.

Contemplations ... *to be or not to be*

The Cauldron

The demons are dancing . . .

I stand guard of my thoughts,
Moment by moment
As I like you
Am being assailed
By the prevailing spirit
Of negativity
That surrounds us.

In the cauldron,
The task at hand
To maintain one's light
Can be an exhausting challenge.

We inject our mind-stuff
With hope and gratitude
That we may feel worthy
Of the small pleasures
Life affords us
From time to time.

We examine our past,
Take stock of our presence
Only to project
In to the future
Of variables and ambiguities,
Making promises,
Declaring affirmations
That tomorrow
Will evidence

william s. peters, sr.

The desires of our hearts,
Of our souls.

In the meantime,
The children, the children
Must navigate and make sense
Of the ingredients
We willingly allowed,
Willfully defended
As the pathway
For them to tread.

Is this the stew
We believe to be acceptable,
Palatable and ingestible
We offer those to come?

Who seasoned this dish?
Perhaps the fire
Needs to be lowered,
Or turned up.

There is but 'One' pot,
One planet,
And contrary to
Some aberrant beliefs,
We all belong
To this same sphere of expression.
We occupy the same cauldron.

Contemplations ... *to be or not to be*

Unfortunately

Unfortunately for us, there is no getting around racism and its stories that have been passed down to us from our parents, grandparents and others within our communities. Life in Amerikkka at times proves to be a continuing nightmare that we cannot seem to escape.

If we want to really be effective in the justice system, first we must stop all the money in politics, particularly the NRA, Weapons Manufacturers and Dealers, then the Police Unions and Private Prisons. We must call a spade a spade, and be diligent and vigilant in vetting our courts, prosecutors, legislators and all public servants to include the police. This is only a start, because bias is learned, taught as is overt racism.

Let us be clear: it is not that I as a Black man don't like White people, no. As a Black man, I do not like many of the 'white ways' that marginalize my culture because of my ethnicity, the color of my skin or anything else that puts me and my people in an unfair and inequitable position. This applies to not only whites, but Asians, Arabs, Jews and any persuasion that takes on a predisposition of who I am, who we are, and acts upon it, or not!

Those who teach hate will reap hate. Those who teach Love will reap Love. Those who attempt to teach both are simply teaching dysfunction, and that is what they shall reap.

We have come to the table many a time, and were, at best, only offered a 'visitor's' seat. It is now time for us to seriously consider making our own table and stop asking 'massa' for handouts to temporarily appease our hunger. There is plenty of table wood, but I am willing to bet it will

william s. peters, sr.

be deemed illegal to chop down our own trees on our own land to build one.

Contemplations ... *to be or not to be*

You

You are my favorite color,
The reason I believe in rainbows,
Because you, yes, you
Are my pot of gold.

You must be the reason
That the birds sing to me,
For the glow of you
Is all about me.

I care not for horizons
And what may come,
For I have you
Right here next to me.

Tomorrow, as they say,
Is but a promise,
And yesterday
Is being forgotten,
For I am blinded this day,
And every day
By the light of your presence,
Your glow.

You are the melody
That gives cause
To my harmony,
And we are the composition
That the masters of music
Sought and seek to express.
Yes, you are my reason for rhythm.

william s. peters, sr.

This breath I breathe
Is laden with the fragrance
Of the makings
Of your heart . . . love.
. . .
I am the Spring,
And you are the reason
My flowers bloom,
The reason for
The bees and the butterflies
Who exude a wonder
That enlightens, evokes
The giggles and laughter,
The souls of the children,
And thus, us all.

You are so much more
Than these simple words,
And I am too simple
Of mind and of heart
To capture the rapture
Of our life-embrace.

I look into your eyes
And I become lost
In the depths of expectation
Of what we may yet become . . .
Unsettlingly delicious.

You are my inspiration,
The summation
Of my elation.

Contemplations ... *to be or not to be*

You, you, you
Silence me, my Angst,

For in your heart
Is where I wish to
Eternally dwell.
. . .
You . . .

william s. peters, sr.

See You in Sinop

I know of your longing
For the place of your dreams,
Past and present,
Where Karadeniz
Kisses the shores.

An idyllic place
That embraces its children
In a charm
That will never cease.

I watch the sparkles and twinkles
In your eyes
And the sprinkles of joy
Upon your face
When you speak of this place . . .
And . . . your sighs
Are filled with a hope
To return some day.

People hustling, meandering
Through the bustling streets,
Visiting the shops,
Shopping for groceries
And other fare
To continue their fair

Pace of living,
Giving way to the symbiosis
Of the common joy
Of the land
By the Black Sea.

Contemplations ... *to be or not to be*

I shall go there,
And await your return.
We shall then embrace
As we walk the wet sands
With naked feet,
Sharing the essence of a love
Found in your heart,
Found in others,
And now, found in mine.

I thank you for this gift.

So, should I go before you,
Follow the path,
The path back home,
And I will once again
See you in Sinop.

william s. peters, sr.

We Do What We Can

We may not be the strongest,
The smartest,
The most able
Or most stable, but
We do what we can.
Don't we?

Life challenges us
To become bigger and faster,
And at other times,
Slower and smaller.
I am not sure about
The shorter or the taller,
But that does not negate
The dichotomous nature
Of our existence, does it?

We are up, we are down,
Over and over again.

Gaining new friends,
Losing old ones
Due to politics, opinions, geography
And death.

Perhaps life is like that proverbial onion
And we keep peeling the skin away
Layer by layer,
Until we get to something usable
Or nothing at all,
While the tears
Continue to fall.

Contemplations ... *to be or not to be*

Some search for and seek earnestly
Fame and fortune,
While others are never noticed
By notoriety.

Some are content
For what they have,
For in their estimation
They have enough,
While others will never
Get to enjoy
That sweet respite.

Some like to invade
The halls of solace
With their noisome presence,
Never caring
Who they may disturb or offend.
Then there are those
Who walk in humble humility
With little or no aspirations
To leave footprints
In the garden,
Or pluck the petals
Off the flowers of life.

Some seek the light,
Some find comfort
In the shadows.
Some speak loudly,
Some voices are softly uttered.
Some could never be quiet,
And speak with excess,
While others are satisfied

william s. peters, sr.

With their inner thinking
And the peace it affords.

Some smile,
Some frown,
Some are stoic.

Some play,
Some work,
All to varying degrees.
Some are minimalists,
Some are excessive.

Some dance,
Some paint flowers on the wall,
And others are the ones
Who play the music
. . .
Me? I love to observe.

I believe
There is an earnesty we all have
To live our lives
In our own way,
Even if 'that way'
Has been adopted from others,
Be they weak,
Be they strong,
Be they smart, able or stable,
Or not . . .

But, when it is all said and done,
Each man, each woman . . .
We do what we can.

Contemplations ... *to be or not to be*

The Phoenix

From the ashes, I rise
That I may plummet into the
Fires of death
That I may rise again.

The cycle of life and death,
And back to life again,
Is an endless one.

We stand.
We fall.
We stand again.
This, too, may appear
As an endless cycle . . .
Until we plummet
Into the fires of death,
So that our souls are enabled
To rise from the ashes
Once more . . . for . . .
I AM the Phoenix.

william s. peters, sr.

Whether . . .

Whether we are in denial or not, whether we identify the source as God, Allah, The Universe, Buddha, Krishna or as other entities makes not a bit of difference. Creation will, and have always expressed its 'self' as its 'Will' . . . sometimes through us, sometimes for us, but always . . . all ways, of its own accord. What its agenda is perhaps is not known, save the great consciousness that we get to tap into every once in a while. It requires not our permission to proceed forth in its quest of the evolution of 'being-ness'. The best we can do is to be silent, be still and observe . . . observe the movement of which we are a part of . . . observe the energy that flows through us, to us and from us as we experience the resonance of life.

Contemplations . . . *to be or not to be*

Alone

There is never a time
When we are not alone!

The decisions we make,
Though influenced by circumstance,
Or things or people
Are still ours to make . . .
Alone.

The thoughts we harbor
Are not created in mutuality,
But within the confines
Of our own minds.

The love we share
Is ours alone to share and
The choice to do so,
Or not,
Is ours alone.

We wake up alone.
We go to sleep alone.
We experience each day alone,
Even in the presence of others.

We live alone.
We die alone.
The journey we make
Is ours alone.

william s. peters, sr.

Yes, you may share much,
As much may be shared with you,
But it is you alone
Who moves the margins
Of acceptance or denial
And all that in-between ….

2 B finished

Contemplations ... *to be or not to be*

Embracing the Wind

Here I sit
Upon my haunches
In my private inner sanctum,
The halls of my consciousness.

I patiently listen
As I await
The coming of the new wind
And what delicacies
It has for me
This day.

There will be gifts
From near, from afar,
Gifts from other dimensions . . .
Thoughts,
Dreams,
Wishes,
Desires,
Insights,
And some admonishments
Which all are much-needed
To fuel this forbearance
I call 'my life'.

I consider and hold dearly
That which has taught me
To listen.
For, in the fleeting silence,
There are many treasures
To be gathered,
To be harvested
By he/she

william s. peters, sr.

Who embraces
The quietude.

I cherish the solitude
And the void
Where noisome things
Die,
And I can discover
That which has
Never been uncovered
Before.

This is why you will find me
Sitting here
Upon my haunches
In my private inner sanctum,
The halls of my consciousness.

I patiently listen
As I await
The coming of the new wind
And what delicacies
It has for me
This day.

Contemplations ... *to be or not to be*

To What End?

Although the light in my eyes
Has dimmed somewhat
From what it used to be,
My wonder has yet
To rest.

The body says "no",
Though my spirit still believes
In my delusional foolishness.
I surrender
To its wisdom.

Chance is behind me,
Before me lies providence.
Where I now am
Is in the arena
Of contemplation and reflection.

The mirror is no longer dark,
For time has taught me
Many a valuable lesson.
And . . . I listen,
For my eagerness,
At times, leads to pain.

Aging is not
For the elderly alone,
For none may escape
The onward assault
'Time' wields

william s. peters, sr.

As a weapon or as a gift.

. . .

Cognizance makes all the difference.

We all were playful soldiers
Sometime beyond the horizon
To the east
That has now overcome us.
I amusingly
Look to the west with consideration
Of all the light,
All the darkness
I have encountered, experienced
In my sojournment.

I ask myself often,
To what end
Shall it end?
Will someone come along
And read between the lines
Of my offered meagerness,
And conjure an edible fruit?

To what end?

Contemplations ... *to be or not to be*

Being Human

For the most part,
With dignity we lived.
Yes, we too, have had
Our ugly moments,
Reactions
And callousness.

We did strive a bit
To love those who we felt
Did not deserve it,
And discovered inner treasures
As a result.

We fought battles
Against our indifference
As we attempted to understand
The illogical
And the stupid.

Compassion has become
Somewhat of an art form
As we have designed ways
To exhibit
Our self-described
Noble character.

Though it is evident
What we are as a species,
Being Human
Is always a challenge,
If we choose
To open our eyes.

william s. peters, sr.

The funny thing
About the truth of it all
Is that we are very adept
At surviving ourselves . . .
Well, most of us are.
. . .
Delusion is quite the valuable tool.

Many times, I sit,
And sometimes, I reflect,
Sometimes, I project
While taking an inventory
Of 'me' . . .
Quite the undertaking, if one
Chooses honesty . . .
But for me,
Before I finish reading
The entire book,
I tire of the brutalness of the
'Self-critique',
But somehow, I
Am OK with me
For most moments . . .
The other moments,
I choose to sleep.

So, here I am,
Still striving for progress,
Seeking, searching surreptitiously
For the path to absoluteness,
And I still have
This abiding feeling
That I am still lost . . .
Sigh! So much for . . .
Being human.

Contemplations ... *to be or not to be*

Just Another Day

It was a dreary day in April,
With dark clouds looming above.

The winds would come,
And the wind would go
With intermittent rain
Falling
Here and there.

I looked to the western horizon
And I saw the promise.
Yes, the promise found
In the skies of blue,
And I knew
That this day
And days such as this
Last not forever

Just another day . . .

william s. peters, sr.

Notes

I brought the water to the table
And sat it down
In front of him,
But I guess he was not thirsty
After all.

I labored to prepare the meal,
Seasoned it to his taste,
But his hunger was lost
In the convolution of confusion
So, he ate not.

Contemplations ... *to be or not to be*

A Reality Check

Even flowers
Don't bloom all the time;

Butterflies were once nothing
But hairy worms;

Honeybees
Do die,
As will you and I.

I always dreamt of flying,
The closest I got
Was a helicopter, and many planes.
Does that make me less sane
To dream of such
Inane things?

william s. peters, sr.

Gardeners

In my lifetime,
I have planted many seeds;
Some bore flowers,
Some bore weeds,
Some bore fruit.
Some were bitter, some sweet
But through it all,
I have learned
That, in some way,
We all are but . . .
Gardeners.

I have observed
The budding,
The blossoming and the bloom
As I sat in anticipation
Of what is to come.

I have not always
Been a diligent one
When it came to weeding.
So, I ask not the question:
"Have not my garden I kept?"

I was a quick one
To taste the fruit
Of Mother's spoils,
Even though I did naught
But sow a few seeds
Here and there.

What have I learned,
When it is all said and done,

Contemplations ... *to be or not to be*

Is . . . that, when that final curtain
Has fallen,
What will be remembered
Is what we left behind
And the seeds we have sown,
And the fruit it bore.
For we, in truth,
Are naught but . . .
Gardeners.

william s. peters, sr.

There Will Be Days . . .

There will be days
When unreasonableness,
Despair,
Melancholy,
And other challenges
Will greet you at the front door,
But these are at most
Regurgitations
Of your doubts and fears
That have come to stimulate
Your greater 'self' . . .
To take charge!

Contemplations ... *to be or not to be*

You Get What You Give

There was a fluctuation
In my time-line called 'sanity',
And I thought you too
Were a true friend,
An authentic human being,
Just as I falsely saw myself.

Little did I know or realize
That we were master thespians,
Able to persuade our audience
That illusion was reality
And reality was as we espoused
It to be.

I do not necessarily blame you nor me,
For the world as it is
Inspires us,
Cajoles us,
Nudges us,
Persuades us,
Then rewards us
To be something other
Than what
We innately are.

I, too, have
Stumbled and fallen
From tripping over the
Cracks and bumps
Of delusion;
Be it induced by 'self',

william s. peters, sr.

Or the world about me.
However, I have always had
This penchant
Subtle longing,
And deep soul stirring,
Begging me to awaken
From this ominous slumber
That suppresses
My greater 'self'.

In this brief moment of light,
This moment of questionable insight,
I understand succinctly
That I know little about
The truth of it all;
That even in my incessant searching,
I comprehend very little
That is lasting,
Other than
That you get from this life
What you give.

I do not complain much,
For I have found a couple of truths
That seem to prevail,
And one of them is . . .
Love has its merits
For the lover and the loved,
And it is much more,
Exponentially powerful
In the equation called
'Reciprocity'.

Contemplations ... *to be or not to be*

Perhaps that is a truth
We all can stand on,
That the laws of creation
Are fundamentally built
Upon the never-faltering scales
Of balance.

So, therefore,
If I may conclude but one truth
In meandering through
This dichotomous subterfuge,
That would be simply
As I stated above:
"You get what you give".

Simple Gestures

I have found that very often it is the small things that make the biggest differences in our lives. Holding the door for someone, a soft hello, a smile, a hug, a touch, a wink. Each of these human gestures are simple, and cost us nothing, however they can have a significant impact on someone else's day, and quite possibly, on their life.

Once we take this fact into consideration, you can not but help to realize just how powerful each of us are to effectuate change. Today, you, I, we all can make a difference. With enough of us moving consistently, collectively in the direction of displaying our humanity towards each other, we will eventually reach the 'tipping point'. How about it, are you ready to indulge in a higher vibration where understanding, compassion, consideration and love are the icons and avatars of our existence?

Today, hug somebody, say hello, hold a door, smile . . . it is these 'Simple Gestures' that make a difference.

Contemplations ... *to be or not to be*

I Dream a Little

I lay my head down
Upon my pillow, and
As I close my eyes
And begin my journey,
Once again as I embark
Upon the pathway to
Where I dream
My way softly
Into the night
Where all the foibles and troubles
Of the day
Melt away,
I realize a poignant
Sense of freedom.

I dream of a world
Where all children are happy,
Giggling and full of song,
Play and laughter;
Every man, every woman
Has shelter
From life's storms;
A full belly,
And a full heart
Where love is always leaking
Out upon our world.

I dream of a world
Without need.
For we do have enough for that,
Don't we?

I dream of epiphanies

william s. peters, sr.

To be realized,
And all the 'ugly'
Vaporizes
As it vanquishes
The illusions we cling to
As our realities and truths.
. . .
I also dream of flying,
Soaring in the skies
Where I can look down upon
A world that is all good,
Balanced and filled with
Equanimity and love.

After some time,
I awaken,
And I rub my eyes continually.
For this is not the world
I dreamt about,
And I realize
That I, you, we,
Dream too little.
. . .
Or do we dream too much
And 'do' too little?

Contemplations ... *to be or not to be*

When We Sang Along

A gentle wind has come . . .
Once again.

The chimes are singing . . .
Once again,
Telling of its presence.

It is April,
No showers or rains
Today, though the sky remains
Grey with no sunshine
To be seen.

Soon, the flowers will
Bloom,
Children will play
In the freshly mown grass,
Frolicking and giggling and laughing
For no apparent reason
We adults can remember . . .
But I remember
The abandon
With which I played
. . .
I still look forward to the budding
Of the flowers.
. . .
I once picked them
From the fields
Where they grew wild.
They were as wild as I was
At one time . . .
Now I buy flowers

william s. peters, sr.

From the market.

Life for me
And many others like me,
Is a cycle
That evolves from
Those days of playful abandon
Into these days of duty
And responsibilities.
Every so often,
A gentle wind blows
And the chimes sing,
And we remember
Those days
When we sang along.

Contemplations ... *to be or not to be*

on me

my expectations have stretch marks,
for my dreams are much bigger
than my reality

my soul has been impregnated
with an unsated
hunger and thirst
that cannot be dissuaded
nor dispersed
by the commonness
of rehearsed mediocrity

i have been in labor
all my adult life,
striving to give birth
to a higher expression
of my 'self'

the trickster of indoctrination
attempts to retrain me,
defame me,
then blame "me"
while holding me back
behind the cloaked walls
of disdain, doubt and deceit,
but they can not defeat
that which is within me,
vying to become complete

can you feel my pain
in having to endure

william s. peters, sr.

the inane, insane, profane
illusion?

i no longer embrace the illusion,
and the muddied pools of confusion
are becoming a bit more lucid
and i see my past delusion
settle on the bottom
where the bottom feeders dwell,
spinning and telling
their stories, their lies
while trying to drown us, they try

i can not listen
nor can i hear
the name of past fears
dancing with the thoughts
i once bought
when i too sought
to fit in

so now . . .
i shed no tears for them,
for these dry eyes
cry no more,
for there is work to do . . .
on me!

Contemplations ... *to be or not to be*

Love Warriors

Love Warriors: The time quickly approaches when we must mobilize and activate our hidden chakras and allow them to blossom and impart their sacred fragrance unto the world. We have been in stasis, awaiting this coming moment when time ceases, and we do our work. The handwriting has been on the wall since the coming and parting of all the Messengers of The Holy. Peace shall forever reign from this point forward, and the light and darkness shall dance together in celebration of the unification of the Yin and the Yang. The quickening will soon be upon us, and the visitor shall come once again to anoint those who are ready. Are you ready?

william s. peters, sr.

Epilogue

About William S. Peters, Sr.

A 2016 & 2019 Pulitzer Poetry Prize nominee, William S. Peters, Sr., AKA 'just bill', has devoted himself to poetry in 1966. Since the day he became a dedicated voice in making his creative expression public–regardless of form, he has held the passionate conviction that the written art is a necessity. The author's spiritual essence reflects in his social actions, all of which serve his efforts toward the betterment of humanity and the easing of its plight.

To date, Peters authored about 62 books. His poems have been published in excess of 230 anthologies, newspapers and literary magazines. In September 2015, the author was recognized as the "Poet Laureate" at the Kosovo International Poetry Festival. For his sizeable book, *The Vine Keeper*, he was awarded The Golden Grape Award. The book was showcased in Rahovec, the poetry festival's center. Being so inspired by this communion of poets, Peters penned a book of tribute, *O Sweet Kosovo . . . Dreams of Rahovec*. This work has been since translated into Albanian by Fahredin Shehu, an esteemed poet and scholar, and was incorporated into the Rahovec School System in 2017.

From the 2015 inaugural formal introduction into the world of international poetry onward, invitations to William S. Peters, Sr. grew in speed and frequency. In 2016, he attended the Morocco International Poetry Festival in Rabat as an invited participant and the Key Note speaker. In 2017, the author's journey continued through a dazzling tour to Strumica, Macedonia; Monastir, Tunisia; Casablanca and Larache, Morocco; Istanbul, Turkey; Rome, Italy; Amman, Jordan; Bethlehem, Mar Saba, Ramallah and West Bank, Palestine, and Chicago, USA. In sum, Bill's presence was, and presently is, being sought out in a growing number of new anthologies.

The author has been immensely inspired in his travels, and composed a large number of poems and prose pieces during and after his introduction to the places of his personal experiencing. Several resulting poetry collections have been included in *Tunisia, My Love* and *7 Days in Palestine . . . the Land, the People, the Blood, the Tears and the Laughter*. Peters was commissioned to write the book on Tunisia. It was launched in 2018 at the Poetry by the Sea Festival in Monastir, Tunisia in the author's presence.

William S. Peters, Sr. is the founder of Inner Child Press International, and currently serves as the CEO of Inner Child Enterprises, Ltd., Managing Director of Inner Child Press International, Executive Producer of Inner Child Radio, and Executive Editor of Inner Child Magazine. He has published many first-time writers from across the globe through hands-on assistance, counseling and guidance, thus introducing a large body of literary work to the public. In its brief history, Inner Child Press International–Peters' publishing enterprise has brought global attention to a multitude of poets by means of official releases and inclusion of their craft in numerous anthologies.

The author's undertakings under his publisher-cloak encompass notable anthology series of global endeavors, including the voluminous *World Healing, World Peace* – published every two years since 2012, and *The Year of the Poet* – a monthly book, as conceived in January 2014 and published every month since. In the latter anthology, The Poetry Posse, a core group of contributors, comprises between fourteen and eighteen writers from various world regions. This publication also features four guest poets each month.

William S. Peters, Sr. has received recognition for his work at large–publishing as well as writing also in the U.S., his country of birth. His appearances on North American radio and television shows are too copious to list here. His poetic work has been published in various countries of the world, including Kosovo, Albania, Germany, Iran, Iraq, India, The Philippines, Taiwan, Canada, Italy, Romania, Saudi Arabia, Jordan, Morocco, Italy, England, Romania, France, and Poland.

The author is known to be adamant about taking time out to share his humanitarian, spiritual and philosophical insights wherever he is invited. He has cited and performed his poetry at a variety of venues, such as summer camps for children, teacher workshops, poetry workshops and classrooms, including an October 2017-lecture to graduate students at The University of Jordan in Amman, Jordan.

In addition to composing poetry, the author has one other life-time passion: to induct underrepresented cultures into the mainstream entity of the "West". To materialize this predilection, he has–among other globally collaborative works, published *Voices from Iraq*, *Kurdish Voices*, *Aleppo*, *Palestine*, and the encyclopedic *Balkan Anthology*.

In his own words: he has been 'building bridges of cultural understanding' throughout his career as a poet and a publisher.

In 2019, William S. Peters, Sr. has authored *Eclectic Verse*, another voluminous book of poems. His creative writings in 2020 include the five volumes of *The Book of krisar*. In 2022, he has published *Unapologetically Black & Blues*. He is presently working on two new poetry books, with multiple additional manuscripts waiting for their turn.

Peters says: "I have always likened Life to that of a Garden. So, for me, Life is simply about the Seeds We Sow and Nourish. All things we 'Think and Do', will 'Be' Cause and eventually manifest themselves in an 'Effect' within our own personal 'Existences' and 'Experiences' . . . whether it be Fruit, Flowers, Weeds or Barren Landscapes!" In high regard of the "Fruits of his Labor", William S. Peters, Sr. wishes that everyone would thus go on to plant "Lovely Seeds" on "Good Ground" in their own "Gardens of Life".

A Selection of Other Works by the Author

available at . . .

www.innerchildpress.com
www.iamjustbill.com

and other fine bookstores

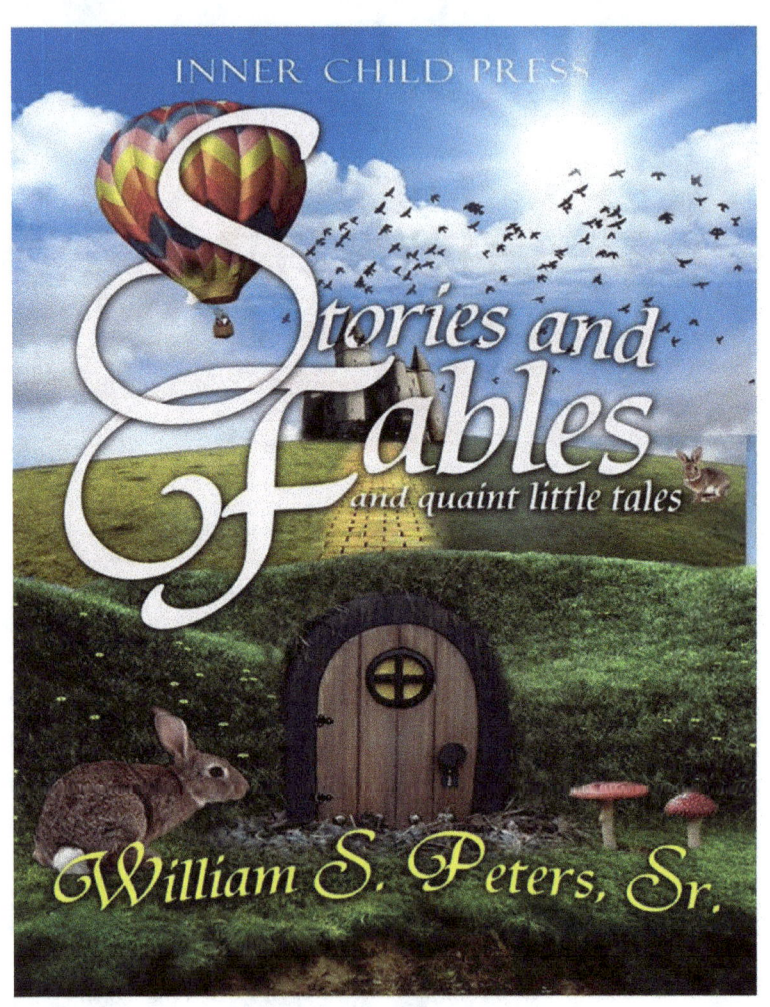

O Sweet Kosovo

... dreams of Rahovec

Poetry & Prose

by

William S. Peters, Sr.

it's all about the Love . . . baby !

william s. peters, sr.

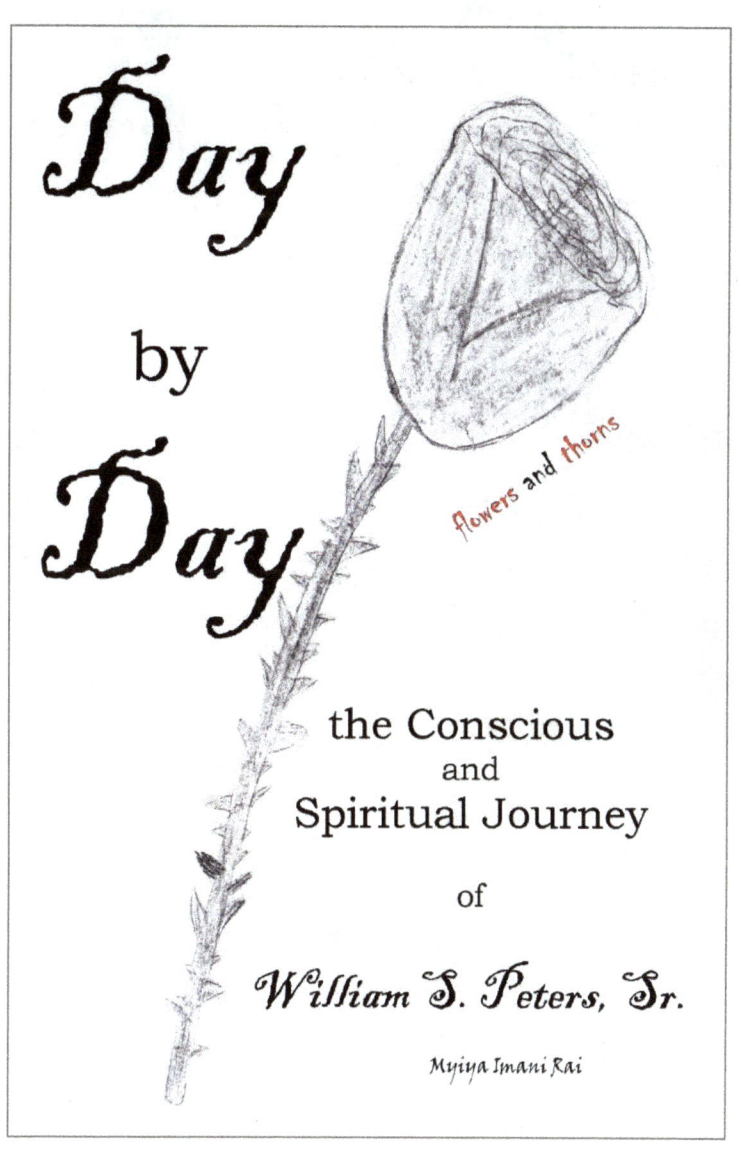

Day by Day

flowers and thorns

the Conscious
and
Spiritual Journey

of

William S. Peters, Sr.

Myiya Imani Rai

Web Links of the Author

Personal Web Site
www.iamjustbill.com

FaceBook
Bill is the 1

Instagram
Bill is the 1

Search
William S. Peters, Sr.

www.innerchildpress.com

Inner Child Press

Inner Child Press is a publishing company founded and operated by writers. Our personal publishing experiences provide us an intimate understanding of the sometimes-daunting challenges writers, new and seasoned may face in the business of publishing and marketing their creative "Written Work".

For more information:

Inner Child Press

www.innerchildpress.com

intouch@innerchildpress.com

www.ingramcontent.com/pod-product-compliance
Lightning Source LLC
Chambersburg PA
CBHW070537170426
43200CB00011B/2456